Learning Spanish For Kids

Author Tony R. Smith

Copyright © 2020 by Tony R. Smith. All Rights Reserved. No part of this publication may be reproduced, distributed, or transmitted in any form or by any means, including photocopying, recording, or other electronic or mechanical methods, or by any information storage and retrieval system without the prior written permission of S.S. Publishing, except in the case of very brief quotations embodied in critical reviews and certain other noncommercial uses permitted by copyright law

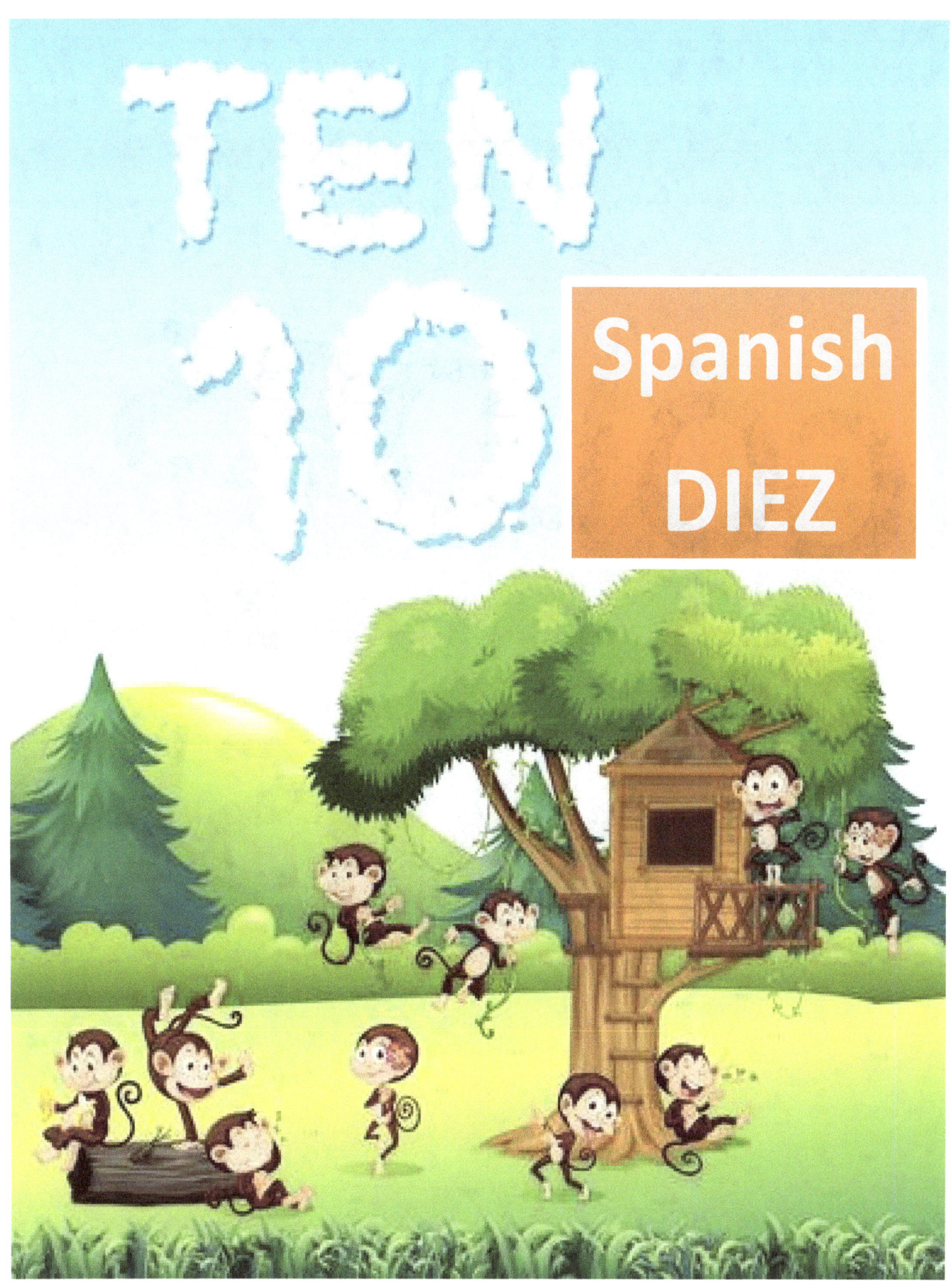

COLORS IN SPANISH

RED
IN SPANISH
ROJO

GREEN
IN SPANISH
VERDE

YELLOW IN SPANISH
AMARILL

GRAY IN SPANISH

GRIS

ORANGE

IN SPANISH

NARANJA

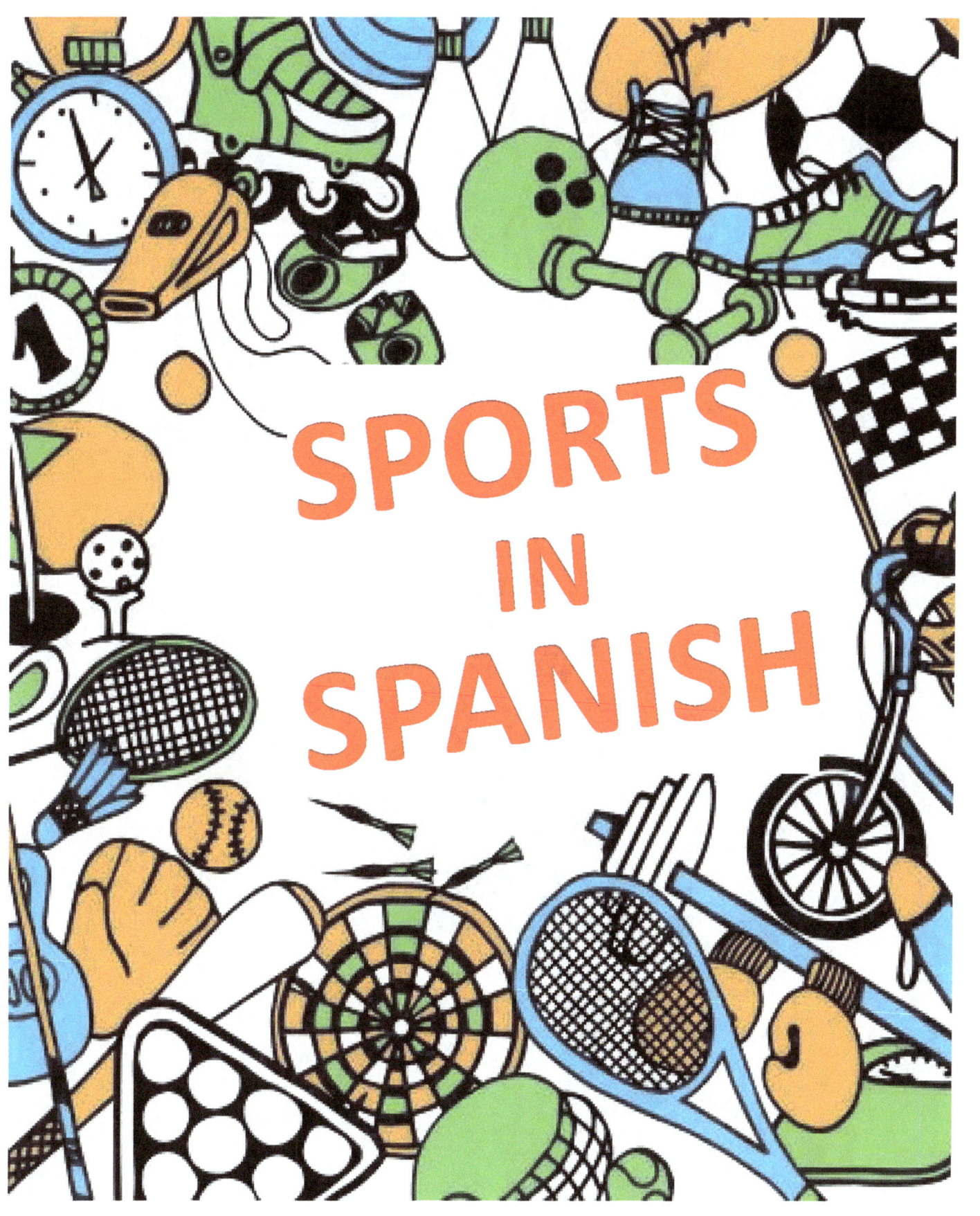

FOOTBALL
IN SPANISH
FUTBOL AMERICANO

BASEBALL IN SPANISH
BEISBOL

BOXING
IN SPANISH
BOXEO

TENNIS

IN SPANISH

TENIS

BASKETBALL
IN SPANISH
BALONCESTO

ICE HOCKEY
IN SPANISH
HOCKEY SOBRE HIELO

SOCCER
IN SPANISH
FUTBOL

TRACK THE SPORT IN SPANISH

SEGUIR EL DEPORTE

NOTES

NOTES

NOTES

NOTES

NOTES

NOTES

NOTES

NOTES

NOTES

NOTES

NOTES

NOTES